BROKEN ROOTS

BASED ON A TRUE STORY

DARICE BROOKS

BALBOA.PRESS
A DIVISION OF HAY HOUSE

Balboa Press books may be ordered through booksellers or by contacting:

Balboa Press
A Division of Hay House
1663 Liberty Drive
Bloomington, IN 47403
www.balboapress.com
844-682-1282

Because of the dynamic nature of the Internet, any web addresses or
links contained in this book may have changed since publication and
may no longer be valid. The views expressed in this work are solely those
of the author and do not necessarily reflect the views of the publisher,
and the publisher hereby disclaims any responsibility for them.

The author of this book does not dispense medical advice or prescribe the use
of any technique as a form of treatment for physical, emotional, or medical
problems without the advice of a physician, either directly or indirectly. The
intent of the author is only to offer information of a general nature to help
you in your quest for emotional and spiritual well-being. In the event you use
any of the information in this book for yourself, which is your constitutional
right, the author and the publisher assume no responsibility for your actions.

Any people depicted in stock imagery provided by Getty Images are
models, and such images are being used for illustrative purposes only.
Certain stock imagery © Getty Images.

Print information available on the last page.

ISBN: 978-1-9822-6466-6 (sc)
ISBN: 978-1-9822-6467-3 (e)

Balboa Press rev. date: 02/26/2021

This book is dedicated to my Mother, My King/ Husband, My Angels, My Sons and My Grand Babies. No Matter The Weather We Will Win & Rise, Crowning... Ancestral Healing, ASE...!!!

Broken Roots is similar to a novel called

The Coldest Winter Ever written by Sister Souljah.

Contents

Part One

MEMORIES
OF CHILDHOOD

CHAPTER 1

My memories of childhood are like a puzzle that I piece together as I write my story. I'm writing my life out on paper with the hope of touching someone else's world, or maybe just assisting them in getting through their storm. One person's story can give hope, clarity, and meaning to another person's existence.

This is my story. I don't mean to be grim or to shine a bad light on any of my loved ones, because God knows I love my family and love to see nothing but smiles on their faces. But the fact of the matter is, I grew up in a very abusive household—with my biological father, Rodney James Dupree, present as our abuser, and my biological mother, Emerald Ann Jenkins, as the wholesome, loving, nurturing, faithful goddess who gave us amazing comfort during those traumatic times. I've always told my friends that when I was growing up, my mother was the angel and my father was the devil.

My parents met at a pool hall in Oakland, California, where they both had jobs. My father and the owner of the pool hall, Manny, were very close friends, so my father was given a job as a manager. But my father also had his own shoeshine business, so he and the owner had a business agreement that allowed my father to run his very lucrative shoeshine business out of the busy establishment. My father was a shoeshine man for the many customers who came to the pool hall and just about everyone else in Oakland, so he knew everybody. His days were filled with long conversations, laughter, business deals, shining shoes, and running a tight ship.

My mother was a beautiful cashier and salesclerk who sold candy, chips, and other junk foods to the customers who came in and out of the pool hall throughout the day. My mother was very shy with the customers but very professional, always getting along with everyone. Everyone loved her. She found herself daydreaming sometimes about her future, how she would someday have this huge, amazing family of her own, a handsome husband, and pretty much what most young ladies fantasized about in their spare time. She was so beautiful.

I know that my father noticed her, and her beauty was probably one of the reasons that he'd hired her. With his aggressive nature, plus being the joker that he tended to be, he put on quite a show trying to get my mother's attention, joking around constantly. They began a beautiful friendship as coworkers that stayed strictly in the workplace, but after about a year, the pool hall closed down due to the owner's sudden death from kidney failure, and they went their separate ways. They probably never imagined fate would have its way and they would end up meeting one another again.

Due to my father's ability to see my mother's virtue, class, unique personality and soul, I'm certain that he was more than anxious to reconnect with this rare beauty he had found but lost. I'm sure he saw in her what most men looked for in a lifetime partner, a wife. He never forgot her, even after mourning the death of his good friend, relocating his shoeshine business, and redirecting his clientele. He always said jokingly, "Elephants never forget," and he had my mother on his radar.

As fate would have it, about a year after Manny's death, my dad saw my maternal grandmother, Sabrina Jenkins, while on one of his business ventures. My dad had been through some sort of training that day that put him in her area. He remembered her face from the times that my grandmother had picked up my mother from work at the pool hall on the days when it would rain. Rodney was excited to see her, and after greeting her, he immediately asked for my mother's phone number so he could get back in contact with her.

My grandmother remembered my mother, Emerald, speaking of him a while back as being her manager, and the pleading look on his face convinced her to give him Emerald's number. My father didn't waste any time calling my mother when he got home that evening. Emerald was surprised that her mother had given him her information, but she was not complaining and had actually wondered from time to time what had ever happened to him. A date to meet up was set immediately, and they got together again, rekindling a friendship that blossomed into a twenty-year marriage. They fell very much in love and eagerly made plans to start a future together.

My mother already had a child named Venus from a previous marriage, and my father had a son and daughter, Sammy and Tina, who were not in his care or his home at the time. My father truly loved Venus as his own, embracing this new child into his life and giving her everything a father is expected to give. Things set off in a good direction: my father took an interest in culinary arts and became a chef, and he and my mother later opened a catering service together that did very well. He was also in the union as an iron and construction worker, so he stayed busy, and my mother pursued a career as a part-time nurse at a children's hospital.

I can't really remember my mother being pregnant with my other siblings or them even being born, but I do vaguely remember a couple of the pregnancies and me enjoying the moments when I could put my hand on her belly and feel the movement of the unborn child. I would get so excited trying to determine if the little lump moving underneath her smooth, tight skin was the fetus's head, foot, or butt, which was always funny to imagine. I can remember lying up against my mother for long periods of time, waiting for any sort of movement from our baby, my sibling.

I think one of my major highs during these moments was being close to my mother and her contentment with me being so close to her. In my family, there was seldom any hugging or kissing. We rarely heard the words *I love you*, but we knew that we were loved and that if anyone on the outside of the family was to offend or attack us in any way, we were protected by a force that I believed could move mountains: my father. My parents gave me six playmates: my sister Ameerah, who is one year older than me; my younger sisters Khadijah, Aishah, and Jamilah; my brother, Malcolm, who is the only boy; and last but not least, the baby, Rasheedah. Together, my parents had six girls and one boy.

My earliest memories always take me back to a white house with green trim on Allendale Avenue in Oakland. This home will be etched in my memory forever, I believe, because there was such chaos, horror, and abuse present.

My name is Malakiah Dupree. I am a Cherokee Indian, Seminole, and African American native of California. I am twenty years of age and currently reside in a jail cell at the Claybank Detention Facility in Fairfield, charged with forgery. I always wanted to write out the story of my life, but I just never had the strength to dredge up all of my family's past hurts, pains, and trauma. Sitting in this cell—cell nine—somehow seems like the perfect opportunity to push through my pain and into my healing.

CHAPTER 2

I believe that in this jail cell is where I truly began my healing, because not only was I finally able to think about the pain I had stuffed and hidden away over the years, but I was now willing to write about the things that haunt me daily. I was now willing to dig through my family's dirty laundry to find out what had happened to me—what had molded me into the monster and angry beast that I've become.

I will begin with my memories of the green house with the white trim on Allendale Drive in Oakland, California. My recollection of events seems to draw a blank concerning any time before we lived in that house. My father, Rodney, was of Cherokee and Seminole bloodline. He had a very rough childhood filled with abuse. He was moved around as a foster child from relative to relative. He never knew his real father, and his mother, being an alcoholic and single parent, tended to abuse my father, often causing him severe emotional problems.

He did the best he could growing up—fighting peer pressure and graduating high school—but my father was an angry man, and he held a lot of his pain inside until one day, all of it erupted, like puss from red and swollen wounds, leaving ugly scars behind. He was also an alcoholic. Although I myself personally never, ever saw him take a drink except for once in my life, his drinking was a huge factor in the destruction of our family.

The green and white house on Allendale Street was set on a good residential block where the majority of the residents were of the working middle class. The neighborhood was very quiet, and you rarely saw much activity except on holidays. Thinking back, as a small seven-year-old child, that house always seemed so huge to me. We spent a lot of time indoors as children.

Behind the main house in the huge backyard, there was a playhouse that was an exact duplicate of the main house. The playhouse was large enough for a twelve-year-old child and five playmates to enter comfortably. Right next to this playhouse was a beautiful garden that my mother worked very hard to create, with carrots, squash, peas, tomatoes, eggplant, and every other vegetable you could imagine growing in a garden.

I remember spending many hours in that playhouse with my siblings playing homemaker. I always had to be the authority, the grown-up, or the parent during these games. I would never play the child or the one being bossed around. I always wanted to be the one telling my siblings what to do in our fantasy world, pointing my finger and making demands, imitating my parents. We would pretend to wash dishes, iron clothes, and do many other domestic household chores.

The playhouse was equipped with a complete kitchen, living room, and bedroom. There was an ironing board that would fold out of the wall, which I liked the most because at age seven, I was not yet allowed to iron my own clothes. Here in this playhouse, in my fantasy world, I could iron all day. This place was a great escape from the main house; I could pretend that everything was perfect and there was no abuse, yelling, or angry faces.

I remember there was a window in the playhouse that gave me a perfect view of my mother's garden. I would stand there and watch over my mother for what seemed like hours. She would always be so at peace during her times in her garden, turning the soil with her hands, tending to the plants, pulling weeds from time to time, and stopping to marvel at her work. Her mind always seemed to be miles away, and I wanted to go where her thoughts had traveled because she seemed so happy there.

This window was also where I sat after the times when my father would have beaten her the night before. I would always be afraid to look directly in her face after one of those beatings, let alone speak to her. We would just go about our daily routine in the home, passing each other with no real eye contact. On these days, I would make a mental note to get out to the playhouse before Mom made it out to her garden so I could hide there at the window. From that window, I could look directly at her without her seeing me. I could look at her swollen face and bruises without shaming or embarrassing her.

I would stand there watching her until my legs hurt and my feet began moving back and forth, trying to keep up good circulation. As my beautiful mother would pull up weeds from the garden and plant new things, I remember thinking that if she was to ever see me watching her, she would hate me for it. I truly thought she would confuse the act of me being concerned with me just being nosy.

I wanted at those times to hold her so bad that my chest would ache. I never wanted her to leave that garden, because I always felt somehow that there in that garden she was safe, with the sun shining on her face, as her hands moved in perfect rhythm, creating life once again. It would melt my heart every time to see her take off her gloves, gather her tools, and prepare to meet the family back in the home. She would collect her things while seeming so broken and unsure about something, but in the midst of her pain, there was always this peace about her. It was as if I could see right through her sometimes.

It seemed that just my eyes and my presence there somehow healed her—just me standing there watching her in perfect peace and harmony, playing with that colorful vegetable garden being nurtured by her hands, made everything all right. It always pained me to see her go back into the house. It tortured me when she would stand and walk back into the garage that led into the main house. After she was inside, I would sit for some time alone, rocking my body with my knees to my chest, not knowing how to process the trauma in my world.

Why? I remember thinking as the tears stained my face. *Why?*

Things gradually got worse. I'd seen my dad stab my mother in the head with a screwdriver, so I had a huge fear in me now for my mother's safety. We were allowed to see the violence inflicted on my mother a lot of times. On the day my mother was stabbed by my father, I remember my father yelling, grabbing my arm, lining me and my siblings up on a long bench under our dining room window, and making us watch as he fought my mother.

This fight went from the bathroom and into my parents' bedroom. This was the first time I had ever seen my mother fight back, and I believe the motivation for her fight was the anger she felt at my father for allowing us to sit and watch this horror unfold.

I recall objects being picked up by my mother to hit my dad with, and my dad taking these objects and using them on her. My mother's screams for him to stop still ring in my ears today. During this particular battle, my mom continued to fight back, but in an effort to stop my mother from hitting him, my dad grabbed a screwdriver from a shelf and stabbed my mother in the head. My sister Ameerah, who is one year older than me, ran into the kitchen to call the police. She was eight years old and had to climb up onto a stool to reach the phone on the wall.

As she was dialing the numbers, my oldest sister, Venus, out of fear, made my father aware that the police were being called. Immediately, my father ran from the crime of abusing my mother and went after my sister, who was now standing on the stool talking to someone. I remember him hitting my sister so hard that she literally flew off the stool and hit the floor.

The sound of my sister hitting the linoleum was enough to make your stomach weak. He yelled into her face with flames of anger pouring from his eyes and mouth. I began crying at this point very hard, while feeling a sense of danger and thinking that at any minute, my dad might seriously hurt Ameerah—or I might be next. I used all off my inner strength trying not show any sign of fear or trace of tears as my father began storming in my direction.

My mother, by now, had found time to check her wounds, and my dad had enough time to come out of his rage. I recall my mother coming out of the bedroom where my father had left her with blood dripping down her face. She walked into the bathroom with the intention to clean herself up further. There was a constant flow of blood coming from the wound in her head that now drained into the sink.

I wanted her to look at me so badly, but my dad walked into the bathroom, blocking my view, and began assisting my mother with what appeared to be care and love. My pounding heart felt a mixture of excitement and relief. Though his words were still harsh, his actions were now calm and caring toward my mother. I believe he now realized, as he always did after the fact, that he had gone entirely too far.

My mind draws a blank about what happened after that

moment. What I do remember is being upstairs with my siblings, laying in our separate beds. I had thoughts of climbing out of our bedroom window, which was two stories high, and out into the cold Oakland night and its mysterious darkness. I wanted to go to my fantasy land—to the magical playhouse in the backyard—and dream of a world far away from here. I wanted to change these events.

I wanted so badly to leave my bed, but I knew that one of my siblings, out of fear, would tell on me, and this would cause new trouble. I never thought for a minute that jumping out of that two-story window in my bedroom would break my little legs and neck. All I saw was an exit, and I believed that if I could just get into that darkness outside my window, just get out and sit in my little play world, occupying myself with fantasies of a life far from here, then everything would magically be okay. Eventually, sleep took me under, where I could take a break from the confusing thoughts that were ripping my brain to shreds.

CHAPTER 3

Checkered throughout the years spent with our father were good times and bad. He loved all of his children, even before birth. From the day we were born, he put us all on pedestals, choosing Arabic names for us that held status and meaning. He described what he felt each time our mother pushed one of us out of her womb and he looked into our tiny infant faces for the first time. Each time in the hospital with my mother—seven times, to be exact—I believe my father saw just how perfect his world really was. He adored my mother, but the hurts and pains from his dark past always seemed to lurk like a monster, threatening to destroy our family at every turn.

One week, we would all be laughing, loving, and living a happy peaceful existence. The next week, he would be Satan's right-hand man, tearing apart and casting to the wind our family's balance along with its much needed structure. This drama usually took place when he would have too much to drink, or maybe he just had a bad day.

During the good times, my dad would go all out, sparing no love or expense, it seemed. He loved going to live Muhammed Ali fights; Ali was my father's favorite boxer, so we always had tickets to his fights. Our family outings included the roller rink, where I would skate with my siblings until we dropped. We went to many live stage plays, ballets, concerts, even religious retreats. We would all get dressed up in pretty dresses, wearing our little mink and rabbit fur hats and coats, our faces full of smiles, wondering what fun was up ahead.

My personal favorite was the time we went to see Disney on Ice. The characters always took my mind far away, as I would watch them gliding across the ice, acting out many different stories and funny antics to excite the audience and make the crowd roar with laughter. I would scream, shout, laugh, and constantly look back and forth at my family members, happy that they were equally enjoying themselves. There were smiles on everyone's faces, and my father was seemingly at peace with us and the world. I don't think we ever missed a show on ice.

My father was a man of many faces, and we never knew what to expect from him. It is clear that he loved us, and not only because of the names he chose for us at birth, such as *Malakiah*, meaning "good queen" or "royalty," or even the material wealth with which he showered us. None of these things are the reasons that my memory of his love is so evident, but it is simply the way I remember him being during the good times—how he would hug us, or his favorite game of picking us up above his head and spinning us around on his shoulders or his back, giving piggyback rides, tickling us, or just dancing to some oldies but goodies from the Solid Gold collection. At those times, I was filled with the sense of what a truly close-knit family structure would feel like. It felt so complete.

I also remember days spent in front of the fireplace, roasting marshmallows with chocolate and graham crackers, sharing loving moments as a family, watching movies, and eating popcorn, chips, and other junk foods (which we weren't normally allowed to have due to my parents being strict about our health and their desire for us to have strong, white, cavity-free teeth). The movies we would watch were never what you would expect. It was always something like *Roots* by Alex Hailey, which was one of my father's favorites, or National Geographic.

My father thought it important to make my siblings and I hate white people for a past long gone. He taught us that we were better than any other race, that we created every race, and that we as kings and queens should never mingle with *white trash*, as he called them. If you weren't Indian or African, you could not be in our presence.

He allowed us to watch African American award shows honoring musical artists or African American actors and actresses speaking on their successes. My father was serious when it came to Indian and African American history and our bloodline. We were not allowed to watch shows like *Leave It to Beaver*, *The Brady Bunch*, or any other white shows, because in his words, "those shows" were a sad and feeble attempt to brainwash our African American young minds and even brainwash some adults. He said that "the American dream was only a plot to sell us self-worth, and we are not buying." He wanted us to be strong and firm in our belief systems, confident in our skin, and proud of our history, dating all the way back to the biblical days and Egyptian times.

I was always taught that all of the events that took place in the Bible took place in Africa, and we were a chosen people. He told us this was why, out of all the other races in the world, we were the only race with a different grade of hair that was shaped like a crown. The curly African hair was, to my father's understanding, God marking us as the original man, the first man ever created.

As he would say, we were the chosen ones. He showed us in the Bible where it says Jesus had hair of wool.

He wanted us to know our heritage and history. He gave us strength, love, and truth in so many areas of our young lives, but his being an abusive alcoholic made it almost impossible for us to grow up properly. We received a lot of mixed messages regarding our self-worth from him, and for the life of me, I could never figure out why, if we were so royal and important, he treated his wife and children as he did.

My sister Venus, my mother's first child from a previous marriage, always took a lot of abuse because she was not my father's biological child. His anger tended to be turned on her more often than not. Venus, though very beautiful, had low self-esteem because of his abuse, and as she got older, it got worse.

Venus and my sister Ameerah were models, so they used to do many fashion shows and events modeling various clothing lines from different Islamic fashion designers. I use to love watching them practice their pivots and turns, always in awe of the way they made the fabrics they wore dance around their bodies and feet. I was always fascinated by their elegance, perfect posture, and poses. Being that Ameerah was my father's biological child and his firstborn by my mother, he would give her encouragement and praise that he would purposely deny to my mother's first and oldest daughter, Venus.

I specifically remember a huge fashion event where my sisters were modeling matching outfits. Ameerah walked out first, prancing and spinning to the sound of the music as we all stood up and clapped so loud that the rest of the audience did the same. They then called out Venus's name to come out and join Ameerah in her matching outfit. My father ordered us to stay in our seats and not clap as my oldest sister came out from behind the curtains.

I was so angry. I did not understand, because I was equally excited for both of them. Not being able to resist the urge, I put my hands under my mink shawl and clapped silently, afraid that I might anger my father if he saw me.

Many times, my father would try to make Venus feel like an unwelcome guest in our home and in our lives. I don't think he ever treated her badly because she deserved it. He just had his own personal mental issues. In the beginning of their marriage, when Venus was the only child, my father was loving toward her. But after my parents began having children together, his actions gradually changed.

Like most children, Venus may have felt threatened by the new baby and maybe showed early signs of jealousy or insecurity during the pregnancy and after Ameerah's birth. My father was bothered as he picked up on Venus's fear. Instead of nurturing her, he turned against her, in more ways than one. Now that he had his own child by my mother, his relationship with Venus was tarnished. His abuse toward her showed in many ways and at many different times throughout our young lives.

The worst beating I remember her receiving was when, at the tender age of fourteen, Venus met a young man at a religious retreat in Chicago. People had come from all over the world to attend, praise God, and sell religious artifacts, art pieces, jewelry, and lots of food. Evidently, this young man was fascinated by Venus. The feeling was mutual, so they exchanged phone numbers.

The young gentleman stayed in Chicago, which was a very good distance from our home in Oakland, California. They would take turns calling each other, and I truly don't believe they knew the damage they were doing by the minute. This, as far as I know, was my sister's first love interest. It had to be love if she was willing to sneak behind the whole family's back to make those private phone calls.

When the phone bill came in the mail, there were numerous calls to Chicago from our home. Being that the rest of us were under the age of eight years, my father knew it was either my mother or Venus. I don't recall how he went about his investigation, but it is clear that he got to the bottom of it. We were all called from where we were playing and ushered up to our rooms. Venus was asked to stay downstairs, which set off a panic to the core of my being. We had no sooner closed the doors to our bedrooms than the yelling began from my father.

At the time, I didn't know if the anger was directed at my mother or my sister. Then I heard my sister let out a bloodcurdling scream that tore through the walls. My stomach got sick instantly, and my thoughts went to jumping out of the two-story window to find refuge or help. I looked at my coat in the closet and thought how easy it would be for me to just put on my coat and shoes over my footed pajamas and jump out into the night. I needed a way out of this house and all of its madness.

It seemed as if her screams went on for hours. I could not understand what was taking so long; her beatings were never this lengthy. I needed to help her. Somehow, I needed to save my sister.

I heard her yelling out to my mother saying that my dad was about to kill her. I didn't know what that meant, but I knew it was bad.

I crept to the door to look out but was stopped by Ameerah, who feared for my safety. My heart was breaking as anger welled up inside my chest. I wanted my sister to come upstairs to bed with us. I wanted to see her now and hug her close to me. I got so sick I began to feel like vomiting.

I must have looked at my shoes and coat in that closet for hours, entertaining many thoughts of escape, until finally my eyes would not stay open any longer and sleep rescued me from the horrors of that night. I remember trying to think of a plan to get to my sister as I drifted off, thinking that maybe if I wet my bed, I would have a perfect excuse to go downstairs to check on my sister while heading to the shower to clean the urine off my body. At least I could see if she was okay—but sleep took me first.

The next morning, I woke up kind of late and realized that I was the only one left upstairs sleeping. Everyone else had been up for some time doing their hygiene and preparing for breakfast. A few of my siblings were already eating silently, and I immediately went looking for Venus. I heard talking as I went down the stairs. It was taboo to wake up and roam the house without brushing your teeth or washing the sleep from your face, so I hurried to do my hygiene while straining my ears to listen to the conversations taking place in the living room. It was hard to hear over the brushing of my teeth and running water, so I made it quick.

As I left the bathroom, I heard Venus talking to my mother, which brought much joy to my heart. I peeked around the corner and saw my beautiful sister lying on the couch with a cast on her leg that went from her toes all the way up to her knee. I had never seen a cast before, so I slowly walked over to the couch to examine this new attachment on my sisters leg.

It turns out that during my sister's beating, my dad had used a broom on her 115-pound body to begin the torture. When the broom broke in half, my dad went into the hall closet and grabbed a wooden baseball bat. My sister's leg ended up broken during the repeated use of the bat on her small body. As she was using her legs to kick him away from her out of panic and fear, a bone in her leg and another in her elbow were broken. This could have also been caused when he had used the broom earlier during her punishment.

After my dad had completed his crime on my sister that night, he had my mom drive her to the hospital, where she was admitted, cared for, and released. The story we were to tell any inquiring outsiders concerning her injuries was that she fell off of her bike. How the hospital fell for that story with all of the bruises on her body, I will never know.

I recall hating myself for not being more brave and helping my sister that evening. It was as if she could read my thoughts as I stood next to her looking in wonder at the cast on her leg. She put her arms around me. As if she felt my pain, she hugged me tight as I cried, feeling her pain as well.

I cried for not wetting my bed (which had seemed like a perfect plan the night before). I cried for being too scared to jump out of my bedroom window to get help, all because I was afraid one of my siblings might tell on me before I could get one shoe on my foot. I cried for not doing what our father had taught us, and that was to protect each other no matter what. I felt I had failed. I always thought as a young child that I could somehow save the world. How? I never knew.

My sister was on crutches for months healing, which kept my father away from her. Until this day, I wonder how she got through such an ordeal, but I thank God that she did make it. My father was her daily tormentor, yet she still loves him unconditionally. Though he is not her biological father, she still calls him Daddy.

CHAPTER 4

I don't really even remember when my father began afflicting abuse on the younger members of the family—meaning myself and my sister Ameerah. The physical abuse only went as far as us two. I can honestly say that there was not physical abuse on a daily basis, but the mental abuse was just as damaging. We all lived in a sort of silent fear of my father.

So much more happened in that house on Allendale Drive, but I draw a lot of blanks due to me being so young. More than likely, I chose to forget a lot of things. One thing I recall is caterpillars being lined up in jars in our garage, waiting to turn into butterflies. Catching caterpillars was a favorite pastime for me. I would put them into old mason jelly jars with a few small branches off of a tree and some leaves for them to eat. I always tried to pick the branches with the leaves already attached.

I don't really know what started this fascination, but I vaguely remember seeing a caterpillar for the first time and someone telling me they were magic because of their ability to go inside of a cocoon and come out with wings. As the days passed, I enjoyed watching as these magical creatures slowly spin a perfect silk sanctuary around their soft furry bodies. They came in so many different colors—mostly red, green, and black, but our backyard was a traveling path for many caterpillars so they were always around.

I would pass the time just wondering what they felt as the silk covered them. Did it hurt as the change took place inside the cocoon, which seemed like the perfect hiding space? I smiled at the peace I knew they must feel, being so safe and warm. As the cocoons would become a home away from home for my friends, I would feel a sort of sadness mixed with excitement, knowing I would have to wait through this amazing transformation for them to become butterflies.

I would keep everyone away from those jars and tell them absolutely no touching. Looking at those jars became a great escape for me. I thought about them at night, wondering what the caterpillars were dreaming, if they were all right, and whether there was enough air in the jars. It was at times like these when it was pure silent torture just trying to get to sleep.

Finally, the moment I'd been waiting for would arrive, when my little projects/friends would come to life again after such a long wait for me (I still, to this day, have a problem with patience).

When it was time, I would stare at the jars in anticipation. The cocoons would wiggle about, swinging in circles from the stems they were hanging from as the butterflies fought to be free. As the color of the wings appeared, I felt as if I could feel wings sprouting from my back. I lived vicariously through these beautiful insects struggling against the silk cocoon of life, begging for freedom.

Finally released from their prisons, they flapped their wings in anxious little flutter motions, testing their new source of transportation. It is funny, thinking back on this memory, that I was always afraid to let them go, so Venus would do it for me. Taking them out of the jar by their wings, she would place them in the palm of her hand, one by one, and toss them into the air, allowing them to catch the wind beneath their wings for the perfect takeoff. These were precious moments for me.

This was always one of the highlights of my spring season while we stayed on Allendale Drive. It's funny how life will spin out of control in the worst way, and then the most simple things will bring you amazing joy, grounding you and giving you a feeling of completion. I believe that this is called *grace*.

At times, things would get so difficult that it was nearly impossible to get close to anyone, so I became a child who loved to isolate myself. I interacted with my siblings, but I trusted my alone time like a best friend and wished I was an only child. What child with eight siblings underfoot wouldn't? As a grown woman now, writing this book, I must say that I am amazingly close to all my sisters and brothers. We have bumps in the road, but we tend to make a speedy recovery every time. My father and mother were big on expressing to us how family was important and should always come first. I thank them for that, because we live and breathe that golden rule till this very day.

CHAPTER 5

I recall one day waking up to the sound of breaking glass as my father tore through the house. In his rampage, he broke mirrors and a few windows. My dad had lost his job due to his short temper, which more than likely was just the last straw for the boss who fired him at the iron yard where he worked. My dad always seemed to get jobs doing construction or iron work, but somehow, things would fall apart for him. He was behind on the rent and owed from the prior months, and a phone call had taken place with the landlord early that morning. We were getting evicted. Things were going downhill fast for my family due to my father's alcohol problem.

There was now six children in the family: Venus, Ameerah, Khadijah, Aishah, Jamilah, and myself. I remember my mother being so stressed out, desperately trying to keep us out of danger, being that there was glass flying and shiny pieces of broken glass in the carpet. Worry filled her face as my father continued yelling out a stream of curse words, threatening to kill the landlord for not giving him more time to get the money together.

He went into the kitchen and grabbed a bottle of honey.

Unscrewing the lid, he began pouring honey into the carpet in an effort to make the house look as messed up as he was feeling. Maybe he just was trying to ease his anger, but he was only making our situation worse, while at the same time showing all of his children bad anger-management skills.

As I said before, my father had a lot of anger within him that stemmed from his childhood. From what I've been told, his biological father's people were sharecroppers and very poor, and his mother's side of the family were wealthy people and felt that their daughter, his mother, deserved better than a sharecropper's son. So they moved away, and he never got to know his father's side of the family or build a relationship with his father because he was moved around a lot in foster care, he was what folks considered to be a bastard child, his life growing up was full of letdowns, broken promises, and abusive situations. He was a dark-complexioned Indian, so he was called a nigger as well as other demeaning nicknames by friends, peers, and family. He became a rebel with the nature of a ticking time bomb. He had a strong spirit but very low self-esteem.

We ended up moving out of the four-bedroom house on Allendale to a smaller one-bedroom home in Emeryville,

California. This new place was a little blue house with a white picket fence that looked perfect on the outside. The inside would have been just as lovely if it wasn't for the physical and mental abuse that began to spread to the younger siblings once we moved in. Now I can clearly see where the extra stress, tension, and drama evolved from once we moved into the new place: there were now eight people sharing a one-bedroom house.

As you entered the front door, you walked into a huge living room, which is where my mother and father slept on a foldout couch. Farther back was the kitchen, which was connected to the dining area. The children's room, which held five of us, was to the left of the kitchen next to a huge white refrigerator. The door connected to the back of the kitchen led to a den where my oldest sister, Venus, slept. There was also a bathroom in there. so she had like a master bedroom, since she was the eldest girl and needed more privacy than the rest of us.

A door in the den led to a huge backyard with a patio deck, picnic table, and spa area, which I loved the most. We spent a lot of time enjoying ourselves in the jacuzzi's warm water, with the bubbles spraying around our bodies. We would pretend to be fish in a fish bowl and swim to the bottom of the spa to touch the glaring lights below.

My father also used the patio area as a shooting range. He would line up cans and bottles along the top of the neighboring fences and then have us children practice shooting the objects off the fence. I remember being frustrated at first shooting the weapons, because they had such a powerful kick; as soon as I pulled the trigger, I would be thrown backward and miss my target. I would sometimes practice with the rifle, but not too often, because not only was the gun too long for my short arms but my shoulder, where the butt of the rifle was supposed to rest as I pulled the trigger, would hurt from the impact of the gun's kick, as it would always throw me off balance.

With my father's constant encouragement and me learning how to position my body, brace my feet, and be very sturdy before "cocking the hammer back" (I used to love saying that), I learned to take perfect aim. Before I knew it, I was knocking the objects off the fence one by one. I loved the feeling and the sound of shattering glass as I hit my targets.

My father used to say that there would be hell to pay if someone messed with his children, and then he would laugh loudly. We would laugh with him just because we were happy to see him smiling and enjoying us. I always believed that he was the most powerful force on the planet.

One day, my father and I got on the subject of the bogeyman. He told me that he had killed the bogeyman a long time ago with a knife, and all the stories I heard about the bogyman now were lies. We started laughing, but I recall at that moment feeling a sense of security and that as long as he was around me, nothing could ever harm me but him.

He was strict about being strong, not showing fear, and standing up for yourself. I recall having to fight a girl named Jada (or Snacks, as she was called, for her reputation of bringing lots of sugar-filled snacks to school every day). Evidently, she did not have enough parental supervision, and she was somewhat of a bully. Jada used to have a lot of friends because of the many snacks in her backpack that she always shared at recess and at lunchtime. One day at school, she got in my face because I was not moving fast enough on the monkey bars. I had my own flow at school, and I was fair as long as you didn't get tough with me or come in my personal space.

I remember jumping down from the monkey bars and telling

her that I was not finished playing. She immediately dropped her backpack and pushed me down. I was a little nervous because she was way bigger than me, and then I remembered my father's words. It was as if I was in a slow-motion picture. All I remember is us fighting, the sawdust from the playground flying around us, with children screaming *Fight! Fight!*

I kept thinking that my coat was too bulky and was messing up the left hooks that my father had taught me to deliver. She was on top of me now, and I could smell her Twinkie breath as she pulled my hair. I was seriously regretting not taking off my coat when someone pulled her off of me, because the teachers were coming in our direction. They couldn't see who was fighting because of the crowd surrounding us, so as soon as I was free from her Twinkie-stained hands, I collected my things and began walking off in the direction of my house. I didn't wait for my sister Ameerah, because that would have meant getting caught by the staff members coming my way.

Going home to tell my father about the fight, I kept trying to figure out what had just happened. I walked in the front door of our house and saw him sitting on the couch. I blurted out immediately that I had been in a fight, and that was why I was home before Ameerah. He got up from the couch and, walking toward me, saw I had a scratch on my face along my cheek. He asked if I had won the fight, and I told him I didn't know.

He then smiled and said, "Let's go see."

We drove back to the school, which was about five blocks away. Pulling up to where all of the children were still standing outside waiting for their parents, he asked me if I saw the girl I had fought with. I didn't. As he was backing out of the parking area, I felt as if he was disappointed in me and upset that we hadn't found the girl.

We were almost three blocks from our house when I saw her big pink jacket bobbing down the street. She was laughing and talking to a crowd of other children. I shouted to my father that she was up ahead, so he pulled the car over without them seeing us. I wasn't sure what he expected of me, but we got out of the car and crossed the street to where Snacks was walking. He told me to walk up to her and put a mark on her face like she had put a scratch on my cheek.

Not understanding, I asked him, "Should I just hit her?"

He said, "Yeah, in the mouth."

When Snacks saw us walking up to her, she stopped with her

head to one side, as if she was trying to figure something out. She seemed different to me now. It was as if she was much smaller now that my father was standing there.

My father stopped at the corner of the block and told me to go get her. I walked up to Snacks and, without thinking, drew my fist back and crashed it into her nose. I was aiming for her mouth, as my dad had told me to do, but the punch landed four inches or more above her top lip, on the bridge of her nose, causing her to scream. She had a look of surprise on her face, as if she could not believe that she had just been hit in the face while an adult was present.

I saw blood and looked back to see if my father had seen the trauma I had just caused this girl. He waved for me to come with him back to the car, and I moved like a solider at war. He was laughing, which was a good thing. No sooner had we pulled off and headed home than he began praising me on my performance. His laughter made me uncomfortable, but I felt like I had won something big, the way he was talking and going on about how I had hit Snacks in the face.

We pulled into the driveway. I hopped out of the car and was heading toward the front door when my father came up behind me, picking me up, swinging me in the air, calling me his little champion. I laughed so hard at that moment as he spun me in circles.

He bragged to my mom and sisters, saying that I float like a butterfly and sting like a bee (words of Muhammed Ali). It was a special, very happy, and victorious moment for me because I had finally made him proud, but it also gave me the mixed message that violence was okay.

I prayed for any good times to last with me and my father, but they never did. On the same night as my famous fight, we all ate dinner, did our hygiene, and headed to bed. My mind was so busy going over the events of that day and how things would unfold between me and Snacks once we were back to school on Monday. I felt good that night, like I was floating on air, because I had never hit anyone like I hit Snacks that day.

I must have been up roaming through my thoughts for hours, because I began hearing snoring coming from my siblings' beds. I still was not tired, but I was feeling very hungry. I began thinking about all of the food in our refrigerator and what I could sneak to eat without being caught. It took me a minute to figure out what I wanted, but before I knew it, I was up out of my bed and headed for my bedroom door, which led to the kitchen.

I listened to make sure my dad was snoring in the front room, then I very quietly opened the big white door to the fridge. The first thing I saw was pickles, which I thought would be perfect. I quickly grabbed a paper towel and slid the jar of pickles toward me. The lid was loose, so I was able to twist it open easily. I grabbed a pickle with my fingers and placed it on the paper towel. My mission was complete ... until I saw the cheese.

I loved cheese. Cheese was my absolute favorite. So naturally, I had to get some cheese to go with my pickle. I decided that it would make too much noise if I tried to find a knife in one of the drawers to slice the cheese, so I just took the cheese out of the wrapper and took a huge bite out of the block. *Mmmm* is what my mouth said. Then common sense told me that I was in big trouble. There was now a big bite out of a perfectly square block of cheese.

Closing the refrigerator, I headed back to my bedroom with a mouth full of cheese and a pickle in my hand. I made it safely back to bed and was enjoying the flavor of the cheese as I crunched the pickle. Then my sister woke up and said she was hot. She got up to plug in our room fan that spun in circles to get the air circulating and climbed back into her bed. I was thankful for the sound of the fan, because it drowned out the sound of me crunching the pickle.

I don't remember falling asleep, but I remember my mother coming into our bedroom that morning and asking who bit the cheese. No one said anything, so she walked back into the kitchen mumbling for us to get up and prepare for breakfast. My father had stepped in the pickle juice I had spilled while he was going to get something to drink that morning before he left for work, and he also saw the bite out of the cheese. He left my mother to get to the bottom of it all by the time he got home. She was to tell me and my siblings that if no one told who bit the cheese, we would *all* get a spanking once he got home.

Naturally, I told on myself to avoid putting my siblings in danger. Waiting for my father to get home was torture. I was not allowed to go outside and play for the whole day. I sat in my room reading book after book from our fairytale collection. It was hard to concentrate on the books knowing that later on that day, I would be in for a painful surprise.

One of my siblings would come in to check on me from time to time, just to make sure I was all right. Up to this point in my life, I had never been spanked by either my mother or my father.

I always had the fear of being spanked, but this would be the first for me.

The night fell, and after dinner, my sisters and I went to relax in the den to watch television. At first, I was distracted, listening and looking for my father to walk in any at minute. Venus, noticing my anxiety, hugged me to her side as we got deep into the program we were watching. It seemed like an hour had passed when my mother waved for me to come out of the den. She said that my father was home, and he wanted me to go to my room and prepare for my punishment.

That is exactly what I did. I jammed myself as far up under my bed as I could go and waited for the drama to unfold. One thing I knew for sure: I was not coming out from under that bed without a fight.

It wasn't long before I heard footsteps coming toward my room, and then the door was pushed open. I saw my mother's white house slippers come in first and then my father's stocking feet step in behind her. He asked, "Where is she?" My mother left to look in the den while my father looked in the bedroom closet.

I was getting scared. I felt that by hiding, I might have been making this situation worse on myself, but I also felt a certain victory for being able to delay the inevitable. My mother called my name as I closed my eyes, hoping they wouldn't hear me breathing. This was the first time I had ever been called by my parents and didn't respond. My stomach was boiling with nervous gas bubbles, and I was sure my parents could hear the sound coming from my belly.

My father was the first to begin looking under the beds. There were three sets of bunk beds, and I was under the last set, with my body pressed close to the wall. I thought I heard my mother say, "She is in here somewhere, but please don't hurt my baby." I'm not sure if those were her exact words, because I was too busy watching my father's feet coming toward my hiding spot.

After slowly lifting the blankets, he got down on his knees and immediately spotted me. My heart was pounding as he told me to get my little butt out from under the bed. I just looked at him and shook my head no. He stood up and began moving the bed from against the wall, telling my mother to grab me when there was enough room. I began moving with the bed, scrambling around, trying to stay safely tucked. But he was quicker than me, and I was dragged by my feet from under the bed.

My dad grabbed my wrists and, with his other hand, began

spanking me with a belt. As he spanked me, he spoke of how I shouldn't have been in the refrigerator without permission at bedtime hours, and how he hated a thief and a liar. I kept my eyes on my mother as he spanked me. She screamed that it was enough and for him to stop. I remember fighting to get away for what seemed like an eternity, until I got too weak and too tired. Finally, they both left the room. I was crying more out of anger than anything, and then out of happiness that my punishment was over.

Soon, my siblings came into the room to check out the situation. In the past after spankings, my older sisters would compare or look in awe at their injuries, which were usually welts from the belt used on them. That day, I had what seemed like a million welts all over my body that puffed up into the shape of the belt that was used on me. They were tender to the touch, and some skin was lifted where there was repeated impact from the belt.

Venus, a constant angel in our lives, went for the medicine kit and made sure that each and every last one of my open wounds was cleaned. We were all silent until my little sister Aishah, who was around four years old at the time and very upset by the whole thing, vowed out loud to us all that as soon as she got as big as

Cinderella, she was going to run away from home. This got a good laugh out of every one of my siblings and changed our dampened moods into a peal of silly laughter. Life was good again, and we were all safely together, which was what we loved more than anything.

That was my first spanking, but not my last. It only got worse.

CHAPTER 5

As a young child, I remember always being hyper. My mind would be moving so fast, and my body did its best to keep up. Patience was my worst subject in life, and I never gave much thought to my actions until after the fact. I seemed to think that my actions and my self were somehow invisible—until I'd get caught doing something wrong, and then I would have to come back to the realization that I was not a supernatural creature and not invisible.

There was an incident on a bright sunny morning where my siblings and I were tending to our hygiene. I finished first, so my father told me to go out into the den and get some training panties out of the dryer for my little sister Jamilah, who was only two years old at the time. I was to put the panties on her, since she had just gotten out of a bubble bath.

When I got to the dryer, I noticed that the clothes were still tumbling. Very quickly, I sorted through the white laundry, trying to find a pair of training panties for my naked-bottomed little sister. I was rushing, trying to find them and get them on her before everyone left me to go outside and play. With my mind on going outside, skating, and starting my play routine, I quickly grabbed the first pair of training panties I saw and put them on Jamilah.

The panties felt dry when I put them on her, because there was still plenty of heat from the dryer in the cotton fabric. I was under the impression that they were dry enough for her to put on, but after running outside to put on my skates, I began a play day that lasted all of five minutes. No sooner had I tied up my skates and done my first stunt on my Rollerblades than my father yelled for me to return to the house. Once inside, I was slapped across the face and told to go into my room.

I didn't know why I was being punished, but I ran off crying, wishing that my mother was home. She was working part-time at the children's hospital and didn't get home until the evening hours. My dad followed behind me, saying how he was watching the Raiders game right then but that I could prepare for a beating for putting wet panties on my little sister.

Evidently, when I went outside, my two-year-old sister went to sit on my dad's lap while he was watching the game, and the discovery was made. The Raiders game lasted for hours, or so it seemed to me. During that time, I tried to figure out how to make my situation easier. I remembered Venus saying that putting a book in your pants or some sort of cushion might ease the pain. So with my plan in place, I fell asleep with a towel and a hardback book stuffed in my pants. I dreamed about how I should be outside skating, and I hated hearing everyone out in the fresh air and sunshine having fun. I hoped my mom would come home early.

I guess the Raiders game was over and the Raiders had lost, because when my dad came for me that night, he was very angry. I was yanked from my bed by my arm out of a dead sleep. I remember it feeling as if my arm might break. My elbow was on fire with pain where he had grabbed me.

I was dragged into the garage and told to position myself over the famous trunk. The trunk was a plastic treasure-chest-looking box that held all of the old toys that we had abandoned for some reason or another. The chest was gold and brown, and during these beatings, we were told to position ourselves over this trunk while we got the punishment coming to us. I had never witnessed anyone else being whipped over the trunk; I assume that it went the same for the others.

At this point, I was praying that my father was too mad to

notice that my hindquarters were shaped like a square and had four sharp corners from the hardback book titled *Snow White and the Seven Dwarfs*. I had fallen asleep with the book in my pants, along with the pink towel I had gotten out of the laundry hamper in my bedroom. Being that my father had been drinking during the football game, he began beating me without noticing the padding. He had chosen an extension cord for my disciplinary action.

Even though I had padding in my pants, I was scared, and the impact of the cord stung my thigh area—but the pain was not the worst. I tried to pretend a loud, intense cry with extra squirming, so it would seem to him as if I was in serious pain. This was all new to me, but I was thinking fast.

Then, about two minutes into my punishment, I was told to stand up and take down my pants. That is when my horror began. After I removed the book and padding from my clothes and pulled my pants back up, I was beat for what seemed like an eternity across my back, legs, and bottom. I recall trying to reach my hands and arms behind me to protect myself, but each time I did that, my hands and arms were set on fire with the sting of that cord lashing over and over like a thousand bees.

My mind told me that I had to get away. Somehow, I came up with the idea of falling off of the trunk and then making a run for the door leading into the house. Squirming to make the fall off the trunk seem as close to real as possible, I put my plan into motion. Before I knew it, I was on the floor, feeling exhausted as the lashes kept coming.

Finally, I was told to get up off the floor. I translated that as "run for the door." Heading for the door on my hands and knees seemed like a smart idea to me—until I felt the heel of my father's shoe coming down on my hand in an effort to stop me. The pain was unbearable, and at that moment, I hated him. For the first time in my life, I felt hate, as the heel of his shoe crushed my little hand. A hate so raw and deep for my father formed inside of me, and it promised to cut through my soul.

The hate somehow made the pain of the beating more bearable. I remember thinking that if he knew how I felt about him at that moment, how much I hated him, it would be the end of me. Holding on to that secret hate somehow gave me the power and sense of control I needed to get through it.

Reaching down, he grabbed me by the arm, yanking me from the floor while instructing me to position myself back over the truck. My mother came into the garage several times trying to stop him, but he would always chase her off with threats of harming her flying from his mouth. Knowing that my mother loved me so much and was there for me at that door gave me the feeling of hope that it would surely end soon.

I recall praying that he would not pull out a bat and break my legs like he did to Venus. As if my father had read my thoughts or heard my silent prayer, he told me to stand up. I didn't know what was coming next as my father stood looking at me for a few seconds. Then he walked out of the door, leaving me standing in the garage alone.

Not knowing what to do, I just stood there looking at his back as he turned the corner into the kitchen. My siblings came pouring into the garage with my mother in front of them. My heart, mind, and body breathed a sigh of relief that my torture was over.

My wounds were the worst I'd ever received. My right hand was badly swollen from his shoe slamming down onto it and also from the impact of the extension cords' repeated blows. The bending part of my right arm where the doctor goes to draw blood was damaged so badly from that thin cord, I could see my vein pulsating through the open wound. That wound came from me reaching behind myself to protect my backside as he beat me. Still today, I carry those scars as a reminder.

I was ushered out of the garage by my mother and sent to sit in my room on my bed, which was a joke, because to sit down caused pain so jolting that tears would flow at the thought of it. I was messed up pretty bad from shoulder to kneecap. The backs of my legs were raw, as were my buttocks and my upper and lower back.

My mom was soon back with the first aid kit to patch me up. She cleaned every wound as my sisters stood in the doorway, watching Mom work her magic powers of love. My mother left in tears as my siblings came in to comfort me and look at my battle wounds. They tried to make little jokes so that I would laugh, but I failed to see the humor in anything anymore. The hate I felt for my father was so deep that I could have choked and died on that emotion alone. It reached up into my throat, threatening to suffocate me.

By the time my wounds were all cleaned up and bandaged, dinner was being served, so everyone began to file out of the bedroom in a line to the kitchen, all of them taking comfort in one another. I was so exhausted that I took to my bed, with no desire to eat. But no sooner had I laid down than my father entered the room and told me to get up and go eat my food. I started to cry, feeling twisted inside with hate in my heart for him.

I jumped off the bed and shoved my arm out at him, telling him to look at what he'd done to my arm and hand. He looked at me with anger, bothered by my blaming him and my bold actions. I didn't see it coming, but I was slapped across my face and told, "That is what you get for not listening when I told you to keep your hands out of the way."

I watched him walking out of the room ahead of me, barking out that I better come eat. I was truly shocked and crushed emotionally. I was so sure that once I'd showed him the damage he had done to my arm and hand, he would immediately be sorry for his actions and hug me with apologies.

As I was coming out of the room, my mother was right there to greet me and take me to my seat at the dinner table. I was very tired and didn't want to eat at all, let alone sit socializing with my siblings. My mom comforted me, telling me to eat as much as I could and then go to sleep. So there I was, looking at my siblings all trying to eat one of the many delicious meals that my mother would make for us on a daily basis.

Afterward, there was my favorite part, dessert. But today, I was far from thinking about any such thing. I was feeling some strange new emotions in my young heart that I never knew existed. Hate, loneliness, defeat, and anger ate at my soul, and I felt as if I was drowning as I sat staring at the hot plate of food in front of me. I couldn't even think of eating.

My sisters were still interested in me showing them my wounds while they slowly tried to balance their emotions as they ate. My younger sisters tried to see, but I showed only the older ones, because to get the younger ones stirred up would alert my dad to come check on us. After dinner, I went right to sleep, while briefly reliving that horrible evening. My anger, grief, and frustration lay dormant. There was so much going on in our lives at that time, but on that very night, I grew up.

I knew for certain that we were in big trouble as a family, and I was right. Days later, my sister Venus came up missing. She just disappeared, which was a huge pill for myself and my siblings to swallow, simply because of the love we shared between us. I just remember her disappearing and never coming back.

BROKEN ROOTS PART 2

Things get much worse after my sister disappears, not only am I molested by two women & a man from our family, but my life is turned upside down as new siblings are born & the abuse only gets more unbearable. I'm left to figure out what most little girls in my situation ponder, "How can I save my family, save us all without my legs being broken or maybe dying at the hands of my father in the process?" I always felt like a Super Hero but Why me? The sexual abuse was very heartbreaking & I will definitely go more into detail about this harsh reality in Broken Roots Part 2.

Also, opening up to my readers about the rebellious teenager I became, dealing drugs, bank robberies, being shot by the police and almost killed during a high speed chase. Yes, I was difficult being I had seen faces change overnight and was now hesitant to trust. As a child, I had seen every spirit, the good, bad & ugly & seen those same spirits turn on me as if I were a problem or mistake, more than likely because of their own guilt. Through it all I learned to isolate myself from the world and it was clearly playing out in many different, unhealthy ways as I began to grow into a young woman.

Part 2 of Broken Roots will show you everything that can go wrong when a child is broken and not given any understanding as to how she must now navigate through the pains, depression, darkness, demands of religion and the self-doubt that lays dormant, always hidden, taking root, leading to a path of trials and tribulations, all stemming from my Broken Roots. Thank You To All Of My Readers For Allowing Me To Share Parts Of My Broken Roots. I am currently working on Broken Roots 2 and see myself having it published by the summer of 2021.

It's been a long journey of healing & I'm so glad to be able to finally share this process with you in hopes of helping you along in understanding your truth, excepting your story & knowing your worth in the mist of every storm.

Part Two

UNCHAINED
PASSION

"Unchained Passion" is poetry I wrote at different points
in my life. Each poem is filled with my truths, my lessons,
my losses, my growth, and my creativity. Enjoy the ride!

Unchained Passion

He acts out the words of a love song in his actions toward me, his thoughts keeping me first and his heart wanting to be one with the beats of mine. I see him watching me, trying to figure out my inner beauty, thinking how blessed he is to have found such a treasure. His love makes me forget about all of the other loves who've held my heart hostage. He is a warrior in the battlefields, forever protecting, loving, conquering, and ruling all that is meant for him. I am meant for him, and only a love this pure can hold me so close that I feel complete. Once again, true love knocks down my doors, promising, committing, breathing life into the places where love had lived but had been lost. Careful to never lose this good thing he's found, he acts out the words of a love song in his actions toward me. As we dance together in perfect harmony, with music and lyrics changing with each new day, our eyes and hearts meet. So rare, but rare is the story of my life. He is all of this and forever loved.

ROYALTY

Beautiful piles all around her—barrels and trunks filled to

the brim with silver, gold, rubies, diamonds spilling carelessly

to the earth. This used to be the wedding gift for a woman

to represent his love, her security. The jewels were for the

abundance of children she would have, the life and love that she

would give freely for the rest of her days. Since the beginning of

time she has been everyone's comfort, nourishment, and water,

pure for all thirsty souls far and wide wherever she roamed.

She earned the title of queen for staying true to her virtuous,

gentle nature that was given to her like a flower, so precious,

as a gift from birth. She was crowned from day one, until age

and wisdom seized her bosom. A legend in her own time, and

not because of what she owned but because of what she was

worth when the wealth disappeared. She was solid, true to

her crown, aiming high, always ruling, voted the leader of the

people in ancient times, very assertive but knowing how to

humble herself as a lady, a queen. Warriors and solders would

chop off the heads of any who offended her space and existence.

Even if she stood alone, she still stood roaring like a lioness, dangerous, protecting, counting heads while calling her loved ones home. Always sharing love, warmth, and a pleasant place to be under the weight of her breasts, holding merit in every way since the day she was pushed out of the magical darkness, the womb of her mother. She remembers riding on horses with carriages of gold in her past life, with her crown sliding to the side as she glided down the paths leading to her royal palace. Indeed, her crown was heavy due to the jewels weighing high on her head. She earned that heavy jeweled crown with her soul's strivings, being quick to show action where it truly counted. There is safety, contentment, and loyalty found in this phenomenal, dependable goddess. Okay, so yes, a seventeen-karat diamond ring representing an engagement bond would be quite a heavy piece on her left ring finger, but trust me when I say a room stacked with barrels and trunks filled to the brim with silver, gold, rubies, and diamonds spilling carelessly to the earth's floor would more accurately describe her worth.

No Fear

Walking through life as if in a maze, never knowing what is ahead of you but always striving for excellence in everything you do, with the intent to change at least one person's life with your story, your heart, wisdom, love, and many gifts of knowing. My ancestors, I hear them calling for me to slow down, my conscience calling from behind. Common sense seeking you out, chasing you as you're rushing, fast forward, through life trying to save the world and its people from trauma, pain, and life's many twists and turns. Free everyone of the envy, hate, jealousy, and also admiration of those with skin much different than mine. As much as we would love to end all of the pain, bloodstained floors, bullet holes in doors, bodies resting beneath earth's cold floors before the age of four, but we are only one, we are only one human.

So we just stay content to be of assistance where needed; stay wholesome in thoughts and deeds, since deeds are the only things that will matter in the end when you are called. Good has always been inside of you, but what is your purpose? You need to know your purpose, because just living has never been enough, just existing is a life wasted, waiting for the next moment to embrace you with an empty distraction. I don't play those games that people play or dance to the same tunes that they are so accustomed to, them walking this globe, performing for their fans and onlookers, playing out glittering, glamorous stories that only appear to have happy endings.

Where is the depth of our elders, the old souls, like a man's footsteps on his own homeland, where he tills his own soil, hunts his food with strength and speed, speaking many languages and ruling empires, dynasties, and the masses with the positions of kings and queens. That is the status they held in their own homeland, Africa, our inheritance.

Did you know that this land, this United States of America, is your land? Being it was *not* Indians who roamed the United States before Columbus so-called discovered America, but it was Africans. Africans had been all over the earth millions of years before a Columbus was even born or discovered. This is your land, but it is not your land? So the authority you play out is not real, just entertainment?

You're on the leash and a lease of this bloody soil?

You being of authority is just a figment of your imagination. You're not seeing that you are being bought and sold every day, pimped by your government. We are at war, so we must stay connected, chakras in alignment, feet grounded and in touch with our roots. Roots that have been planted in this rich, dark soil long ago, my DNA. These roots run so deep, so very deep, all of the way back to the beginning of time, like the world of Atlantis. It is our DNA that is saturating this bloodstained soil, not Indians'. This soil was stained by the blood of our ancestors by colonizers. We cried for our children as our ancient history was ripped from our understanding and our grasp. Though our history was buried and hidden away for generations, its living power always continued to move forward, with steps motivated by the first and original heartbeat. An African goddess carried the first heartbeat, but we are all one heartbeat, beating together.

This is all I've ever known, to be one with those around me, staying whole, staying true to my purpose and my love for peace. Reaching out my Mexican, African, white, and Chinese children, saying, "Can you see that it was me? It was I who created you? It was I with my African blood that gave birth to you? I gave life to this nation. Can't you see that we are all the same blood, we are family, we are one? Can't you see that there is a divine reason why I continue to flow happily through this maze like clear, clean water, purifying all that I touch, quenching thirsts for miles around, always knowing that I am here as a creator, a blessing, and as long as I submit to being guided, molded, inspired, and loyal to the forces that I can't see, then I stay royalty …

REFLECTION

It's like I've been there and done that, so I'm not impressed
with much. Though if you're talking about yoga, I'm impressed,
geared up, and ready to go. I've had it all from houses, clothes,
bags of money stacked under my house that came from
bank robberies, drug deals, or many a street hustler's profit.
No matter the source, it was all in black plastic bags under
the house. The boats, luxury cars, and keeping up with the
Joneses was never a problem. Though me and the members
of the big face incorporation had never even robbed a bank
personally, we were a part of the organization. The problem
was, I found that with all me and my husband had materially,
he was really the only thing that brought me pure joy and
happiness. The money was always at a risk of some sort, and
I would have given it all up just for him.. The money brought
me worries, not only because there was so much of it that
I knew it had to be a sin ticking like a bomb, just waiting
to explode in our faces, but also because I remembered the
stories my mother had told me as a child about doing the
right thing, living by laws, codes and standards. Umm, yeah,

but there it was, stacks of sin under our house, in big black plastic trash bags thrown carelessly one on top of the other.

Always we had the most vicious dogs in the yard, on patrol to protect us from any false movements. We both held reputations and titles that kept anyone from even thinking about offending our perfect place of sin, our fantasy of peace and serenity. Anyone who knew us, boom boom, knew what it did around there. There was a program, a system, and you didn't fuck with our system while we were fucking the system. That is how I lived, trapped, unaware, and spoiled by a life that taught me that the world was mine.

All I had to do was bat my eyelashes, red and blue forever showed me loyalty, and I didn't even have to choose red or blue. I was red and blue, and I went anywhere. If I just snapped my fingers or threw a tantrum (whichever you preferred), I could have you killed. I thought the world owed me something, and I wasn't taking no for an answer. I told myself that my requests were not complicated but very simple. I was an easy person to deal with, and I wasn't being extreme with any of my requests or demands. I mean really, I'm not asking for much, am I? Plus the world owes me. Years later, I still believe I am a simple person and don't ask for much, though I've definitely had it all. Yup, been there, done that, and of course, damn, I still want what I want, when I want it.

I definitely hate that I ever had to learn what a car breaking down felt like or what it felt like to live life like the common, everyday people. Those worrying-ass nine-to-fivers, ugh. But I do love that there is a life with less sin, people who live good lives not only with their hearts but with their deeds intact. Without good works, without good deeds, the hearts will die. Going through life now in this current moment in time, living without the luxuries and fabulous, sparkling trimmings of my past here now in my present, I'm learning new things like endurance, patience, faith, work, and things that promise me true heaven on earth or wherever I go. I'm doing more mentally and spiritually to grow this soul, constantly molding this phenomenal design.

Unfortunately, this means that my money does not come in big black plastic trash bags these days, but it's going to be okay, simply because I'm very adamant and holding my position no matter what kind of strong wind hits me—through tornados, hurricanes, and sand storms. In truth, I will be carrying on, holding it down, keeping it simple, forever impressed with yoga and its magical connecting power and the calming effect it has on me.

AMONG WOLVES

Sitting here in this place, this space that was given to me the day love gave birth to my soul and my body. It comforted, guided, and held me until I grew to know more about my existence. My heart and actions said to them, all whom I've encountered, that I wouldn't let the grass grow under my feet. That motivated part of me has always been there, but it was those moments when the heart realized its true potential to love without fear.

Even though fear wasn't ever with me during birth, I still know about it. I think about it like it happened to me, though I carry no fear within. I am fearless like a child, all smiles and wide-eyed innocence, so what is it about me that scares others? I'm not dangerous. I do love living on the edge, of course, with lots of structure, morals, and values but no limits, if that makes any sense. I exercise my right to express myself anywhere, with a strong voice so that you remember me as one you can depend on to speak loudly, clearly, and articulately while staying connected to the cause and purpose, not losing my way as so many have in the past.

What is the purpose of living amongst wolves? I was taught
by the best Bay Area breed, living with many schools of
thoughts that kept me within my boundaries, but of course
never having any limits when you are amongst wolves. I
possess a love that has only known to be treasured like a
fragile package carefully handled. Broken hearts are foreign
to me, like the Chinese and Japanese language. I only know
to be cherished, while everyday I am in return cherishing
the ones who love me, surrounding my loved ones with my
colorful magic, a dance so creative, just loving and loving
over and over again simply because it is long overdue.

Due to the laws of this divine order, due to my celibacy and
honoring my crown, my love is a gift to the one whose heart
I choose to share. I'm bringing back the times of kings and
queens whose love stories have been written in history: a gift
for us both, eternal. I crave to have him kiss these lips—
lips that go years at a time waiting. I'm so glad to finally be
letting him be the last king to kiss these lips on this starry
night. Yes, it was my choice, with no hesitation. I had fallen,
I loved him, and I'm really fine with that. Being he showed

me that my lips can be a portal for his love, that my lips are

precious, and so is his love for me. He knew I was queen,

he saw me, he knew I was a brat queen from day one, he

knew I was made from love. Now we are here sitting in this

place, this space that was given to us as love gave me the gift

of life in him, and I'm grateful living amongst wolves.

GRATEFUL

Life sure can have you guessing what it is all coming to with the senseless tragedies of our times messing with our minds, forever changing winds, making it nearly impossible to see what is up ahead. Though everything is clear and it has always been, we are still unsure. In the end, I can say I'm a goddess, a genius, a channeler creating and supporting the waves of positive energy flowing through our atmosphere. Our universe needs this part of me, and I am connected to it all. Connected but sometimes rejected by those who don't know that we have the same purpose and are on the same team. Excepted by those who love quality, and not in just what you wear or drive but the kind of quality that stands the test of time, the kind that the wise speak about. Open your minds and spirits, because some opportunities come along, allowing you to fulfill your purpose, but they may only come along once or maybe twice in a lifetime. I'm a rare breed, to say the least.

The fall season is already here? Where did the time go? Gotta stock these shelves for the winter, and I am truly grateful to

be able. Like I've always said, "A boat can't sail on dry land."
I try to stay in the water where there lay pureness of nature's
jewel flowing, beauty littering the ocean floor, with nothing
but blue skies for miles in the distance. So transforming,
smelling the peace in the air as it rushes away any thoughts of
troubles on land. Away from it all. This is what I am running to
embrace: the change. Passing time waits for no man, and I am
so grateful for the way I was allowed to love those I've loved.

So the ball just keeps on rolling, can't stop, won't stop; it
is a must that it all comes to pass. Rotation. The earth has
taught us this rule from the beginning of time: rotation
and changing of seasons to keep the balance. Are you still
pushing against the natural order of things trying to create
your own world outside of this one? Rotation, stay with it.

Motion: so much to be done, but it is a pleasure to do it. No
matter what the obstacle, I know I will get through it. Times
gone by are not my focus, but keeping the pace in this race,
making time and space in this place for spiritual, financial, and
mental growth. So much to be done, but it is a pleasure to do it.

GROWTH

There is a better way to treat life, since it treats you so well. I mean, if you were born with two legs and two arms, then you are ahead of the race. But then again, some are still left behind. If life has been good to you and you are reading this right now, you have sight and vision from a soul that the great mother blessed. There is a better way to treat life, since it has treated you so well. You can hug a tree, call your mother, help old ladies across the street, open doors every day for your soulmate, tip the waitress, make someone's day just a little bit easier with a smile from your striking face.

Can't you see how the fruit from the trees of the great mother's labor is already cut for you, slices sectioned off for you pleasure and enjoyment, fruit already perfectly cut beneath the peel's protection, all just for you? Oranges, tangerines, apples, pears, grapefruits, strawberries, kiwi, sun-ripened cherries, perfect, red, swollen, so sweet, all just for you. Treat life good so that you can say every day you've given just as good as you got. It's called being grateful.

Purity

I'm in love with the fact that my heart hasn't changed after all of these years. I'm still full of laughter and joy that flies high on huge, soft wings, never wanting to land. I still love the simplest things in life, like reflecting on fragile moments when I was a child and how I would get so excited when I saw a ladybug, and how I still feel that same spark of joy today. Butterflies also have me captivated that way. They have a power to ease my mind's worries and woes. Oh, and hearing sounds of the waters on the beach and the insides of a seashell will always be a one-of-a-kind winner.

I'm in love with the fact that every time I've loved, it has been pure or not at all. No hugging, no kissing, no rubbing my back unless you were ready to carry infinity like a torch, never to be passed on. Can you imagine the guys who ran from me when they saw my skirt didn't rise and my mind didn't blow with the ever-changing winds? They still run from my virtue, they run for the hills to find victims who are not as skilled in thinking outside of the bullshit box.

I credit myself for being able to see the bullshit before it even hits the fan. I'm in love with the fact that I still have the strength to lift others who need a helping hand, or they just can't seem to stand to see their own worth and beauty, so I share my strength with them until they see we are all the same in value.

Yes, I shine in others as they shine in me, and I am in love with that, being love comes for free. I'm in love with the fortune I found when placed on this earth, an abundant collection of priceless jewels like myself, my family, friends, and lessons I've learned. Oh, and don't forget prayer! Now I sit back and look at all that I am and all that I have. I am in love with that. I'm in love with the fact that my heart hasn't changed after all of these year, and I'm still here crowning.

ANGEL'S MESSAGE

Then he said, "Wait, I'm not finished." Don't be fooled by what

you see in that world down there, honey. We were blessed! Just

like I told you before, nothing or no one has held my heart since

I laid eyes on you. Being you have such a gentle heart, some

things may hurt you more than they hurt others, but woman, I

want to tell you this: just as you can't stop the sun from shining,

rising, or setting, you can't ever change the love I've vowed to

you and you only. Can't you see, baby, where I left my heart?

May 5, your birthday, was the morning God took me

from earth and gave me my wings. I can see things so

much clearer from up here, honey, and you have my world

spinning like a top in the palms of your little hands. I

do not wish to take that from you, and I hate the day

that I ever dishonored your love by the mistakes that I

made on earth. Yes, mistakes, baby; huge mistakes.

Dealing drugs, bank rolls? Yeah, I spoiled you rotten, but

all you wanted was to praise God. Instead you were always

busy loving me. Nothing could ever change what we shared, and I took all of those memories with me when I left. I also took my love for you. Not even the evil, lies, jealousy, and deceit from other people's attacks ever threaten to detour our love. It stayed right on course for fifteen years, standing strong until I left you. I'm so sorry, but I'm an angel now, and I can see everything so much clearer from up here.

You are still a keeper, a winner, a prize, a one-in-a-million chance of a lifetime. Without you walking with me on earth, honey, I probably would have left sooner. You gave my life meaning, flavor, class, style, trust, and promise. I kiss your life and your world with my heart, and I take you, my precious, above all the beauty of the world. You can't stop the truth, and my love will just keep on shining through. I'm going to check on our children now, but if you need me, lady, just think of me, and I will be right there. I promise!

PROMISE

Don't ever forget how much I love you, woman. I love you very much, so what makes you think that I would turn my back on my queen? Don't play with me, lady. It's not even real to think that way. If it was my choice, I would be right there with you in my physical form, but now I'm a spirit, an angel. I spread my wings wide and fly high every day just so I can watch you and also watch everyone else who may be watching you.

I can't imagine hands, lips, or love other than mine touching my wife. I protected you as a mother's womb hugs her unborn child. You are really a rare jewel like no other; you truly possess magical treasures, woman, and not just between those loving, faithful thighs. Yes, baby, now I know that your body is only for love and not play. I know and see so much more now that I am an angel. You were so faithful to me. Oh my precious wife, now I know that you have never lied to me. You kept your skirt down like a queen and your eyes on my back when I walked the earth. I could not have asked for anything more, because true love is what I found to be the strongest force in the universe.

You used to ask me, would I ever give you up? Man, I used to get so mad at that question, because how would you feel if I forgot how much you've loved me? Or how would you feel if I doubted your love? How would you feel if I let the value and quality of our love hang in doubt? So now you're asking me if I will ever give you up? A boat can't sail on dry land, and baby, I'm a simple man. Truly it is not fair, baby, to treat a true love as if you are unsure of its merit, worth, value, and truth.

Even now that I am an angel, high in the clouds, I'm still following you around, standing by your side every minute of every hour. If you ever feel the need to question my love for you, just look into your memories. Look into your mind. Look into your heart. It is amazing, baby, I am now in heaven preparing a beautiful home for us, with gardens filled with your favorite flowers in every color imaginable. Trust me, it's beautiful, baby, but don't be in too big of a rush to see it. Remember those miscarriages you had? Well, those babies you lost are here with me. Take your time; don't play with this life and don't ever forget how much I love you. Close your eyes and just hold my love in both hands, honey, because it is all eternally yours.

TRUTH

It is the real truth that you carry close to your soul when no one is in the room. Like a ghost, your truths haunt the very spirit that you entertain. Like a child in a candy store, eyes drinking in the many sweet colors swirling together like magic on a stick, rainbows and stars in big shiny jars, *mmm*, come take a lick. It calls out to you as your spirit plays and lounges in the delusion of forever bliss. Real truth does not play or have a moment to think of a plot, because real truth is already there, well planned out, just staring you square in the face, but you can't see it. Don't be fooled by the pretty cavity-causing colors gleaming with sugar behind the shiny glass cases or the plastic bold neon candy wrappers. They're just for your entertainment, to advertise, fooling you, dazzling your senses. Don't smell the sugar as it rises from my skin; instead, try to hear my truth. That would impress me.

Today, the fresh morning air has my attention because it flows in perfect motion with the natural design and order, where my mind vacations often. It is the real truth that opens your heart, even when it has been broken, abandoned, and closed for business, traveling alone for some time. I know you. I know who you are. You are that trusting soul, trusting in the joys of giving more than you have ever trusted in the regrets of not giving enough. Real truth stands true even when the chips are down and the odds are strongly against the you. Truth is ever-winning.

What is the purpose of truth? It is here to do for you, to serve you, if you only let it. Stand in guard of your truth and be a living reflection of your unimaginable worth in every moment. It is the real truth that carries us on wings we can trust, never failing or falling short. Real truth from "a real one" …

Give Back

The earth will support me and all that I do, as long as I treat her with kindness. Throughout the years, we have killed her, robbed her, shamed her. It is the very meaning of the word *contentment*, where there lay gratefulness and hope. The earth is my support system and has been since the first day my heart beat, the first days of me running barefoot across her sacred, brown, nurturing, abundant soil. So in return, I must begin speaking for her, being her daily advocate, being that I am made from the earth.

Look at me; can't you tell? Just look at how we vary in different colors of browns, golds, many hues and shades so beautiful that the sun anticipates and marvels at how its rays can stretch forth and bounce light off of our magnificent design, like the precious jewels buried deep in the earth's womb, magic compatible with our DNA. Grateful that melanin, different skin tones like the soils and sands of every land imaginable, faithfully respecting the earth's constant loyalty to me.

Today I must speak up for my old friend who is always
loving, giving birth to new possibilities, because God
forbid she just stops spinning, and we all as a civilization
go flying into outer space, or her waters flood her round
perfection until all life ceases to exist. Imagine the peaks
of her mountains shaking so violently that her abundance
becomes just leveled dust and ashes. Real thoughts!

Thank you, Mother Earth, for giving me birth, breathing life
in me. Great mother, through you the hands of perfection are
on me. Thank you, deepest waters and oceans, as you continue
to travel, sparkling, flowing from heavens up high, the God
realms, and down below to purify me and all that you touch.
I am so very grateful for the delicious feasts that you grow,
piling high as mountains to please our eyes, our lips, our souls.

If we want our earth to help us, we must help her now!
Let's treat our dear close friend with the honor, trust, and
love she gives us daily. Give her your full attention, oh you
of the gods, for we are soon to go back into her womb to

hide once again, hugged by the truths of her ancient stories and history, so long ago gone and passed away. Thank you, Mother Earth, for tracking my footsteps. Like the stars in the galaxy, you have been my guide. I thank you!

As I Found It

I think I found her, or maybe she was sent by an angel,

so really she found me. She is here forever, and I am

all she will ever need, the one she constantly thinks

about. She is so scared, fearful of the love that she has

for me, because she knows that now I hold her heart

in my hands, but she loves me without hesitation.

I think I found her. Yes, she is here, and she has been here all

of the time just waiting for me to see her crown, waiting for me

to see the treasure I'd found in her. She is my queen, a jewel,

not a one-in-a-million kind of of deal but a once-in-a-lifetime

kind of find that you don't gamble away. Yeah, must be nice!

But why does she love me so much? Where does all of

her love for me come from, what depths? Maybe it comes

from the deepest parts of her, which means her love is here

infinitely, teaching, nurturing, shining just for me, giving

me her forever, like a goddess in a bottle here to grant

my every wish, if I could only rub her the right way.

Maybe her love comes from a law that had been written way before her time. Maybe she was sent to save my soul after many lifetimes, as I also make it my life's sole purpose and journey to save her in every way possible. Together, we save each other. I think I found her, a perfect gift from the great mother, sent to find me. Yes, we definitely found each other, but I think I found her.

CARE

I'm soaring in a zone of contentment; not letting the could'ves, would'ves, and should'ves of life hold me back. With the threats of suffocating my drive and motivation, mutilating my ambition, disfiguring my passions, and everlasting desires to raise to a higher ground, flying, conversing with other souls that are compatible with my movements.

I'm soaring in a zone of contentment, knowing that I'm cut from a different cloth, so I can't be tempted to play with those who call me outside into the streets to run, in the sun, having tons of fun with them. They beckon me to come closer to meet with them, but they are no different than dangerous poisonous snakes—like rats, hungry dogs, and scorpions watching me, their bodies crouched low to the ground, teeth bared, eyes squinting, watching my every footstep, waiting for me to slip off my journey's path. They hold out their hands to me, thinking I don't know what they hold in their palms. They offer me roses with thorns that prick my fingers. They want to see my blood draining from my body as they laugh and play, dancing around me, beckoning, taunting, tap-tap-tapping outside of my windows. What I hear in their laughter sounds like pure joy and complete happiness, but I know in my gut that something much deeper is waiting to devour me like in the childhood stories. I'm Little Red Riding Hood, and the big bad wolf is approaching me, disguised in my grandma's clothing.

If I heed their call, if I play with them, they will leave nothing of me but my bloodstained clothes on the damp, cold earth. I'm soaring in a zone of contentment. My legs won't open due to my values and purpose. My back won't bend due to this metal rod of truth that supports all of me, my insides and my outsides, my back and my front. My legs won't open, but I sure can dance. Just turn on the music and watch as I make love with a passion that captivates all whose eyes can see, those whose souls are looking in the direction of my magical performance, the rising and falling of these heaven-sent movements, with a body so flexible and limber it bends willingly to the music. I'm a born dancer, but I can't dance with those standing and waiting outside my doors, sliding up and down every dancehall floor.

I'm tempted because I see one man that I would almost give up my soul for, just to grind my soft innocence against his love and lust for me. I'm so tempted, but I can't play with them; I will surely get hurt. They want to hurt me. I see it in their eyes. But why? Who could hurt a flower? If they only knew that by plucking the flower from the soil for your personal gain, you caused it great pain. Who would volunteer to step on this African violet, crushing it underfoot, boot heels grinding out its royal dark purple hues and magnificent fragrance into the cold, hard concrete. Those standing and waiting outside my door are very familiar with stomping through radiant gardens, trampling and mowing down the fragile beauty of creation as it struggles to grow through the earth's soft, damp soil. There is only one flower left, only one flower left, a rose growing through the concrete. I must protect it; I must protect her; I must protect me.

So I'm soaring in a zone of contentment, knowing that if I play with those standing and waiting outside my door, I will be stepping out of my league, abandoning my morals and values, my boundaries set by the laws of man. I will always in my mind's eye see that one man whom I would

have loved to grind and dance with all of his life and mine

until the sun would rise and fall for the last time, never to

be seen again. I'm tempted, but for my protection, for the

safety of my sacred garden and my gift of innocence, I will

just continue soaring in this zone of contentment, being

sure, without doubt, that the winds will carry me safely

to my destiny as long as I do not stop on the path of my

purpose to play with them standing outside my door.

DESIGNING ME

When I look in the mirror, I see a masterpiece, molded
and designed to perfection, to say the very least. I see eyes
honest, humble, and true, with morals and virtues for all to
see, shining brightly through me. There is something else I
see as I stand here looking at me. I see dreams manifesting,
coming closer to my destiny. I see a lady who carries the
weight of the world on her shoulders because she wants
to help and love all those who are hurting and heal those
who've been damaged by their past and present situations.
I see her passion to change nations with her steady truth
as she moves forward through the land's bloody soils.

She is constantly overlooking, ignoring, and seeing past
those who hate her for no other reason but the color of
her skin and that she walks tall and talks and moves as a
queen. Those who see her God-given beauty look down
their noses at her, but at the same time they are competing
to be her, trying to outsmart her, trying to make her hate
herself because they hate themselves, trying to act as if they

don't see that her beauty literally comes from the galaxy. The universe is her twin and lays within her DNA and her soul. She is intimidating even on her worst day.

I've seen a woman, a queen, a lady who has never envied, hated, or shown jealousy, but she is always ready to teach everyone love at the highest degree. This lady, she is right here standing before me. Yes, she is here with me right now. Do you see her?

Well, I finally see her, and this mirror does not lie. Yes, she is a masterpiece, molded and designed into shape, perfected by the hands of time, a blessing and a gift to all who share in her spirit and space. She carries the grace of a child, the spirit of a goddess. Truly, she is divine. When I look in the mirror, I see the beauty of my soul's design staring back at me, and I cry with joy because this mirror does not lie.

PRICELESS

These are the cards I've been dealt, and I'm happy to say that I'm grateful for the challenges. But through it all, of course, triumph and victory are musts. At the end of the day, there is this wonderful place that we all want desperately to find. This special place should be where everyone is welcomed, with everyone having everyone's ultimate desires and goals in mind. Oh well, only in a perfect world, I guess.

I'm always counting my deeds and trying to cover up any bad one with a good one. It is like jumping from foot to foot. No one is perfect, but we all should just be grateful for the feet we have, the lips we lick, moms calling you daily, or tea when you're sick. It is the little things that plant the seeds. This is without a doubt how the bigger things grow.

We're blessed, so be content deep down in your heart's warmest places. It is priceless, for this is the place where our meaningful existence on this planet means more than what they say it is all about. Am I going to fast? Am I missing a beat? With my beautiful soul jumping from foot to foot but always ready to smile, loving life for what it is.

Now, I will always be a go-get-what-I-want kind of girl, but I will also have faith knowing there is always more than one way to skin a cat. Yes, there is always another way. This is me; I'm walking my path and baring my soul. Thank you for your path crossing mine, because together we are traveling, making oneness whole again, meaning it is all as it should be. These are the cards I've been dealt, and I'm happy to say that I'm grateful for this moment to relax in time, where my heart is filled to the full and my wings stretch far and wide like the rays of the sun—open, open wide. Let's just pray I'm heaven-bound, God's presence manifested!

BLUNT WORDS

My loyalty and love don't come with a price. They aren't based on what you drive, wear, or spend. Money can't buy you loyalty, and my love is not for sale. You learn a great deal about the loyalty of others when you are down or in a bad situation. Since the beginning, loyalty has, through the test of time, run empires, dynasties, armies, countries, and nations. It united those who had loyalty to another together in one place and time.

If loyalty and love are truly in your heart at any point and in any moment, then loyalty should always be present. What the world calls *love* comes in all shapes and sizes, and loyalty does not play the same game as love. So don't be worn down by love lost, because as you'll learn, for some, it's all a game. Keep your love always ready and your loyalty forever on post, so that when things get real, you will stay calm and remember what matters most.

You mean to tell me that if love was not free, you would hold
it back? Would it begin to shine brightly, showing just how
much loyalty you lack? If love wasn't free, you would take
it back? I say it again loudly, just to be clear: my love is not
for sale, but it is always here. I live by the code of loyalty,
and I'm prepared to put up a bloody fight. If loyalty is not
returned to me, my love still stands solid and pure. Though
my physical presence may become absent acceptance, I shall
endure. What the world calls *love* comes in many shapes and
sizes. Loyalty is not the same, so don't be fooled by what
you see or hear, and watch your damn back in this game.

LADY

You have to be doing way more than that to impress me.

Don't be mad when I don't follow your way of thinking.

No, never that. And okay, I won't judge you, but don't

get mad when I don't let you change my crown into a hat

flipped back on a thug's head, not knowing where they

are going from the lives they once led. I love me and who

I am. I'm truly rocking with that. So Imma do me and

you do you, but don't let me catch you talking behind my

back, unless you are hating, which will make you a fan.

I represent a true queen with my ankh in my hand. Even

when I'm broke, I'm still a part of this plan, and I'm not with

your worldly ways. That always gets out of hand. I'm a leader,

an entrepreneur, yeah, I got it like that all day, representing

the word *lady* in a new-millennium-type major way. So stop

talking with that green man named envy. Forget yellow-belly

jealousy and all of her friends. Stop all of your Louis Vuitton

and fake Fendi, because when the lights come on and it's all

said and done, we all know I'm truly one of the real ones.

MAGICAL

I was still loving him when I saw him standing there. My feelings hadn't changed a bit. It was supposed to be a night out on the town with my girl, but it turned into a night of me wanting nothing more than to be with him, kissing him, holding, loving, and doing him. It was supposed to be a night of fun and working my perfected, practiced arts out on the dance floor, but it turned into a night of silent tears, happy memories of him being who he is in all of his glory and truth.

I was still loving him when I saw him standing there; my feelings had not changed a bit. He had changed in his appearance a little. He had put on a little weight and cut off his hair. But none of that was anything but a fleeting thought, because my king was standing right there.

He has the body of a man I want to get to know better, the smile of the man I can ride with forever. He is the sugar in my tea, the caramel on my apple, the sun on my skin, and the light of the moon in my eyes. He takes me places without moving, our bodies a magnet. Together we travel within the love that is clearly between us. I don't want to be without him, but I will do what is written in the laws of order, what is written for this time. In the end, I can always say that my love is one of the realest loves, a love most people won't ever experience or know.

I was still loving him when I saw him standing there. My feelings had not changed a bit. It was supposed to be a night out on the town with my girl, but it turned into a night of me wanting, craving, respecting his love, eternally respecting his love for me. But I keep asking myself, was it just my imagination? Yes, it was. It was all in my head.

OUR PATHS CROSSED

What happened to his life? It seems to be lost in time with all of its twists and turns, its pains and disappointments. What happened to his dreams, the place that used to be where he spent much of his time trying to figure out the perfect way to execute his well-thought-out plans? Where did his life go? It was here just a minute ago: full of possibilities when there seemed to be no hope, making something out of nothing, the inventor of traffic lights and boats. Educating scholars, waking the souls that had traveled amongst the sleeping for centuries. I'm looking for his life that somehow got away. I want to help him find his lost youth that was trapped in a tight glass cage too long, years gone, threatening to shatter at any movement not articulated by the voice. Where are his choices? The spirit is trapped while the body roams free, still clinging to life and its many opportunities. Now here we stand, and my only question is, what happened to his life? What happened to his dreams?

HEAVEN-SENT

To my wife, family, and friends:

There are things I'd like to say,

but first I'd like to let all of you know

that I arrived from my journey okay.

I'm writing you now from heaven,

where I dwell with God above,

where there are no more tears or sadness,

there's just all of this eternal love.

That day I had to leave you,

when my life on earth was through,

God picked me up and hugged me close,

saying, "Son, I welcome you."

God told me to have a seat

and that it was so very good to have me home,

that my loved ones who I'd come to adore

would follow later on.

He told me that he needed me badly

as well as many others,

as part of his much bigger plan

to save our earthly brothers.

Because there was so much work left to do

to help and guide our mortal man,

we sat down to have a very long discussion

about how we would execute the plan.

Yes, I'm in the God realms,

so please don't be sad because I'm out of sight,

just remember that I'm with you in the morning,

your afternoons, and nights.

Though if you should ever meet someone

who is hurting, down, or feeling low,

it could be me, so lend a helping hand as you continue on your way,

knowing you made someone's day.

If ever you're walking down the street

and you've got me on your mind,

I'll be walking in your footsteps,

only half a step behind.

If you're ever laying in your bed

thinking on how we spent our years,

I'll be right beside you like a soldier

to wipe away your tears.

When you feel a gentle breeze of wind

upon your pretty face,

it is me giving you a passing kiss

and a heavenly embrace.

Though remember, if you can help someone

whose heart is in sorrow or pain,

then you can say to the great mother late at night,

"My day was not in vain."

At the end of the day, I will always love you from wings on high,

soaring through this beautiful land above.

We'll be in touch very soon, but until then,

God sends his love.

Soul Surfing

When he speaks, he wakes up every part of me. When he looks
into my eyes, he wakes up parts of my mind that have been
asleep for years. He holds me with his words of knowledge
and wisdom. He touches me with his sincerity and truth.
He kisses me with late nights full of reflection and laughter.
His eyes lead to a path where I can travel, discovering the
depths of us with his every thought, wishing and dreaming.

Did he come to late, or is he here too soon? We don't want
to separate, we don't want lose this moment, so we just
agree to stand still. We stand still holding each other with
arms and hands that wait anxiously, waiting for the law
to pass that will allow us to heal one another from past
pains with each touch, stroke, bite. Oh yes, right there …
Now stop. Don't move. Are we there yet? Well, let's just
pray that we are on our way to love, to forever, together

PASTIME

Watching me is his favorite sport, as he thinks to himself, "Amazing is she to bare her soul to me." He wants me, but time has abused his heart. He holds trust for no woman or man.

His daughter from a past relationship told him last night that she is gay, but he already knew it. It seems she's always been that way. She told him that she and her gay lover were planning to give him a grandchild. Did he give her enough love, or has he been looking for love all of his life?

He wants me, I know he does, but he's afraid to bare his soul to the world, letting others know his true passion for peace with me, living in my arms, in my heart, in my truth. The world has titled him as a boss, a baller, and all about his paper. He likes his titles. He's earned them, but he also knows that a title doesn't define him. Yet he gives up everything for those titles and the worldly things that come with it, day in and day out.

The world can't see that he loves God, he loves truth, he loves quiet nights in front of the fireplace, sipping a cappuccino with his guard down. The world can't see that he wants a good wife who won't ever spin around a pole with her precious vagina, her baby-maker, wide open, on display for all of the world to see. He wants a woman who loves him only. The world does not care about that or honor his desires, but I do. The world doesn't care about him or his needs. The world is a selfish HIV-infested bitch who wants him to entertain her with his sin.

The hos, money, houses, cars, clothes that he claims to need in order to fit into society don't really hold more value in his life than his love for me, but yet every day he chooses these things over me, even over his own soul. He wants me, I know he does; watching me is his favorite sport. But he can't bare his soul to the world, vowing his love for me, so he will just continue watching.

FREE

When your mind is so cluttered and there seems to be no way out, when your eyes want to close in hopes of rest you've dared to dream about, when your hands itch to execute all that is in your heart, to complete all the things that are the depths of your desires, building possibilities, opportunities, showing the path to others, clearing the ways for travel with those same hands that still itch to do more, don't be a sissy, don't be a punk. Move whatever is in your way, with all of your strength, push it down, punch it, be aggressive.

This space is too small, like a little box. I need room.
I need to be able to open my arms wide to embrace
all of our homeless, our youth, our elderly.

There's a sixteen-year-old boy named Steven. He was the dope boy who had dope fiends for parents. Then there is a seventeen-year-old girl named Jamilah who works at the Gucci outlet. She's successfully graduated high school, she's a dancer, she is called beautiful by everyone she meets. While in college, she's majoring in performing arts, but next week she'll find out that she has HIV. No dreams of babies later. Engagement rings will now be a fantasy. She loses her drive now just fighting to stay alive. I hate that part. Give me space to move. I need to breathe. I need to open my arms wide to save her.

SOMEONE'S WATCHING

This poem I wrote in 2002.

Over one hundred thousand beautiful eyes

of different colors, shapes, and size,

watching.

Taking in the good and bad,

not leaving out one part of me,

watching.

I wish I had a dollar for every set of eyes I've seen

today, yesterday, and tomorrow,

watching.

What is it that they're looking for,

patiently waiting to see from,

and will I please them all,

watching.

Do they see something inside of me that I fail to see?

I think if I saw what they are seeing,

I'd spend all day looking at me,

watching.

I've been under the microscope for so very long.

These eyes numbered by the thousands are a part of my life.

I could not imagine being without them

watching.

And yet every night I go to sleep,

I have never, ever heard even one little peep.

I've never seen anything as silent as these eyes,

watching.

They hug me till I'm happy or sometimes crying.

They make me dream of things to be, saying things like,

"You are far richer than your eyes can see.

I feel the warmth of love and sometimes the scowls of heat

saying, "Don't let the grass grow under your feet,"

watching.

I would not give up these beautiful eyes

for all the luxuries of the world. Why would I?

Oh, and the best thing about them?

They are the window to the soul, always constantly

watching.

Two sets of eyes are a link to them all;

making me feel a thousand feet tall.

I pray for years, a life that joins us all,

joining us together so that we can formally meet the calls

of my angels, my someone

watching.

PATCHWORK

Sometimes in life, we follow a heart

that's been twisted, stomped, and shattered apart.

We live off of feelings that others made us feel,

not realizing that now our own actions have no appeal.

We take all of our negatives and, like quilted patchwork,

we take the traumatic, ugly, bad memories

with all of our twisted needs

and stitch them together neatly until our fingers bleed.

It could be the past lover who treated us so very bad,

or the best friend since childhood who we thought we had.

It could be the woman in church who forever steals our glory

or the child killed by a drive-by before he/she even had a story.

Maybe the neighbor who's always drunk, with her badass kids,

always taking her abuse for things they never even did.

The drug dealers, the users, and the prostitutes you read about,

who are trapped in a life so carelessly lived,

they cannot find their way out.

The bus driver who laughs as he speeds up his bus

and passes us at the depot every day,

the glamorous cars and boats we buy

from crimes that do not pay,

the newspaper that is delivered on our wet lawn every day,

the grocery clerk who snatches our money

and never says, "Have a good day."

Some of our patchwork is of places we've roamed;

I would know, because I have patchwork art of my own.

I had sewn it together so tight and so neat,

So I could display my pain for every soul that I'd meet.

I'd moon over my patchwork with tears and sometimes care,

running my fingers over every neatly stitched square,

thinking how so many things in life were just so unfair,

until one day I noticed as a mother, friend, and wife,

I was letting my patchwork determine my life.

With such a large quilt to cover my sun,

I failed to see where my life ended or begun.

I began to look at my patchwork more thoroughly with care

and noticed that faith, forgiveness, and patience weren't there,

but fear began to fill my heart

when I acknowledged the lack of prayer.

The more I've looked, the more I've seen

that where I should have been grateful or loving,

I was greedy and mean.

Frantic, I grabbed the scissors and began cutting,

chopping, pulling all of my patchwork apart,

realizing that it was no longer a magical or valuable work of art.

I pulled it apart until there was nothing more

than colorful shapes, patches, and threads covering the floor.

I looked all around in total distress,

trying my best to find a way to clean up this embarrassing mess.

I didn't sweep them up and throw them away,

because the pieces were real to me,

and I might need them someday.

Confused and bewildered, I started to pray,

something I had not done for forever and a day.

I let the Lord know that tonight I was having over some guests,

and that there was no way in time I would be rid of this mess.

I bowed, crying, my head low, with my hands on my face,

too confused within myself to even look at the place.

With my eyes closed, tears staining my cheeks,

I felt so very weak and out of control,

feeling that cutting up my patchwork was not all I'd done;

I had just cut into pieces of my soul.

When I finally collected my emotions and looked up with a start,

I noticed that my patchwork pieces

were now mended into a perfectly shaped heart.

At first, I began to panic and tremble with abundant fear,

because I knew without a shadow of a doubt

that no one else was here.

But then the ancestors spoke to me,

and the message became so clear.

For me to show the love of a goddess in whatever I do,

to have faith, forgiveness, patience,

and love my whole life through,

clearly the patchwork mending is not up to you.

I took the newly stitched heart-shaped quilt,

folded it neatly, and put it away,

happy to begin preparing for my guests coming over that day.

But first, I must stop to pray.

By the end of my prayers, I could honestly say

that no matter whatever evil would pass my way,

no matier how much sorrow I saw in life today,

no matter how many late bills I had to pay,

no matter how many hurtful games I saw people play,

I would let God do my patchwork mending

and tell that grocery clerk who snatched my money

to have a good day!

Just Do It

Why me? Why him? Why her? Why anybody?

Why ask why?

Who did that?

Why does it matter? It's done.

Can anybody help me?

I can, but I won't, because if I help you,

you might do better than me.

Huh? I don't get that.

What, you don't get the truth staring you right in the face?

Well, just share your story with another,

and maybe they won't get it either.

Then you both can figure it out.

Huh? But I don't understand.

I know you don't. Truly, you won't.

But there is someone who will understand,

so I will wait on them.

Now why is that baby staring at me? I'm sure he sees

something that I can't see, passing through my soul. Maybe

he's looking at my entourage of angels. I hear an army of

angels walking my way, and I see their huge wings flutter

in the mirrors of that baby's eyes. So why is that baby

looking at me? I've come so far, and I don't know why,

but I didn't make it this far alone, so why ask why?

Slow Down

When he died, he looked at me and said it would be okay,

but as he flew toward the heavens, we both knew it would

not be. The winds heard our singing love, they recognized

our silent cries, and they turned him around, sending him

right back to me. So I never move too fast so my angels

can keep up. Never move faster than your angels can fly.

COMFORTER'S SONG

When somebody dies, a cloud turns into an angel and flies up to tell God to put another flower on a pillow. A bird gives the message back to the world and sings a silent prayer that makes the rain cry. People disappear, but they never really go away. The angels are up there putting the sun to bed every day. They wake up the grass and spin the earth in dizzy circles.

Sometimes you can see them playing, dancing in a cloud during the daytime when they're really supposed to be working or on their way to complete a task. They paint the most beautiful rainbows and also the sunsets. They make waves splash and tug at the tide. They toss shooting stars and listen to wishes from you. But when the wind sings the sweetest songs, they are whispering to us too: *Don't miss me to much, my loved one. The view is amazing and I'm fine. Yes, I'm doing just divine.*

LOVE WON'T LET ME WAIT

I sit here wondering why love holds me so tight. Is it because it thinks I might get lost in life's twists and its turns? Well, I guess I might. Might love recognizes me as a personal friend? Is life so loyal to me that I feel guilty when I don't give the same freestyle love in return? I rest on love. It holds my hand as I scream, "Lord, why is this happening to me?"

Love understands my bills, my unhealed wounds that threaten to become pus-filled, painful, and infected under my watch. Love heals my wounds while I rest. Love always is around me; love never goes astray. I even have to respect tough love when it says, "Don't fuck with me today." What would I do without love? I've learned that it is more important for me that I give love, being love is never too busy for me, so my love shall never be too busy for love.

NO AIR

I stroked my angel's wings softly, and then I watched them

grow. Kasimah breathed her love to Aaron that night as she

watched him go. Maybe her angel wings would not grow later.

They sprouted only when he touched her, but when he was

gone, he took heaven too, but grateful his love stayed infinity.

Pure Bliss

When he walked into, or shall I say magically appeared in my world, it was as if I knew, but at the same time, I didn't know. Life had already shown me that while my heart and mind were a definite prize for any man's life, at the same time and in the same breath, my heart and my mind had failed me. They were both making choices that were not in my best interest, leaving me like a wounded animal, hurt, bruised, crying out in pain, scars on my body where I had been branded by the demons of someone else. They weren't my demons, but I carried the proof of their existence.

So when he walked into, or shall I say magically appeared in my world, it was as if I knew but at the same time I didn't know. My, my, my, he is so fine, and like a sponge, I'm soaking up his mind while standing behind the counter at my job, counting dimes. He at the same time is tearing down my signs saying *Stop, I'm on the clock*. His words are taking me on travels through ancient times, as he's thinking how refreshing it is to completely unwind and be a part of her beauty if only for a minute, maybe an hour.

But then an hour passed, and he was still standing here at my workplace, now helping me with customers. He was great at first impressions. His eyes said that he was comfortable in his skin, living the life that he was in, but that in the end he wanted to be comfortable with me. He wanted to win with me. His words were like a brother or a special friend humbly welcoming me in. His posture was like a king, his light amazingly bright. His intellect had so many different levels and dimensions, so our conversations just kept taking flight.

My day shift was almost over; three or more hours had passed. My boss was upset, being I'd had a visitor all day, so he was constantly on my ass. But as always at my jobs, I am forever running the show. So ignoring my employer, I completed my dialog with this stranger. We said our goodbyes, then he left.

Months passed, and I hadn't seen him again since then, but here he was once more at my job, greeting me like an old friend. As the hours passed, again we were trapped in time, exploring the deepest depths of our souls and minds. He flew me over clouds as I took in the view. He walked me through a sea of rainbows as the many colors stained my skin and my shoe. I almost faded completely out of sight when I embraced the many shades of blue.

Then we approached these golden gates, and he told me that within himself, he held the keys to the throne of my heart, and that to the heavens is where he was taking me. *Ring, ring, ring,* my spirit reenters my body when I hear the bells knocking against the doors, letting me know that I was still at work and more customers had just come into my store. Damn, okay, that ruined my dream, but putting on my professional face, I waved to the customers, giving them my grandest smile, saying, "Hi, may I help you find anything today?"

He obviously sees that I'm busy, so he says goodbye and is on his way, looking at his watch, saying how it is getting late but that he'd just bought a house. He wants for me to see it one day and how he's planning to have me decorate. My celibate thighs and watchful eyes were not falling for that mess, so at best he could take me out on a date, being our conversations were so damn great, but that was it. Who did he think he was talking to me with that house-decorating shit? Well, he will learn just like the rest that I'm the best. I don't settle for less, and I'm definitely not the one to be lifting up my dress, trying to impress the masses, or shall I say, asses.

Well, one date turned into two dates, then three turned into four. He was a gentleman, pulled out my chairs, and opened every one of my doors. I heard him say he wished for rose petals so he could litter my path and steps on this marble floor. He called me goddess. He knew my many names. He took my picture numerous times, so I began to do the same. Who was this king so trusting to show me his heart on his sleeve, letting me see this longing in his eyes? I swear it was hard to believe. He respected my wholesome ways and everything about me, and there was nothing about me that he'd missed.

It had been almost eight months of us steadily dating, and we had not even shared one little kiss. We were building a friendship, a solid foundation where love

could truly survive. We were erecting a fortress

around ourselves and planning the rest of our lives.

To make a long story short, we are married today.

We planned a New Year's Day wedding, and we were on our

way to honeymoon in Egypt, placing our feet on African

lands, making promises of forever. I even drew our names in

the desert sands. Happiness is our fortune, and abundance

overflows eternity. We have honored our vows from then

until now, so tell me what you know about infinity.

When he walked into, or shall I say when he magically

appeared in my world, it was as if I knew but at the same

time I didn't know, so I took a chance and stepped out on

faith. I gave my heart without any limits. I leaped high

touching the sky and landed in my destiny grace.

Stay grateful and true to your spirit. Live out loud!